ISBN 978-0-484-36705-9
PIBN 10154669

For support please visit www.forgottenbooks.com

THE
School for LOVERS,
A
COMEDY.

As it is Acted at the

THEATRE ROYAL in *Drury-Lane.*

By WILLIAM WHITEHEAD, Esq;
POET LAUREAT.

LONDON:
Printed for R. and J. DODSLEY in *Pall-mall*;
and Sold by J. HINXMAN, in *Pater-noster-row.*
MDCCLXII.
[Price One Shilling and Six-pence.]

ADVERTISEMENT.

THE following Comedy is formed on a plan of Monfieur de Fontenelle's, never intended for the ftage, and printed in the eighth volume of his works, under the title of Le Teftament.

The fcene of that piece is laid in Greece, and the embarraffing circumftances depend on fome peculiarities in the cuftoms of that country. Slaves likewife, as is ufual in the Grecian Comedy, act as confidantes to the principal perfonages. The Author, therefore, hopes he may be excufed for having made the ftory Englifh, and his own; for having introduced a new character, and endeavoured to heighten thofe he found already fketched out. The delicacy of the fentiments in Philonoe and Eudamidas, he has inviolably adhered to, wherever he could infert them properly, in his Cælia and Sir John Dorilant ; and would willingly flatter himfelf, that he has made great and not contemptible additions to their characters, as well as to the others.

Thofe who will give themfelves the trouble to read both pieces, will fee where the Author is, or is not indebted to that elegant French Writer.

TO

THE MEMORY OF

MONSIEUR DE FONTENELLE,

THIS COMEDY IS INSCRIBED

BY A LOVER OF SIMPLICITY,

THE AUTHOR.

PROLOGUE.

As it was intended to have been SPOKEN.

SUCCESS makes people vain.—*The maxim's true,*
   We all confess it —— and not over new.
The veriest clown who stumps along the streets,
And doffs his hat to each grave cit he meets,
Some twelvemonths hence, bedaub'd with livery lace,
Shall thrust his saucy flambeau in your face.
Not so our Bard : tho' twice your kind applause
Has, on this fickle spot, espous'd his cause :
He owns, with gratitude, th' obliging debt ,
Has twice been favour'd, and is modest yet.
Plain Tragedy, his first adventurous care,
Spoke to your hearts, and found an echo there.
Plain Comedy to-night, with strokes refin'd,
Would catch the coyest features of the mind :
Would play politely with your hopes and fears,
And sometimes smiles provoke, and sometimes tears.

   Your giant wits, like those of old, may climb
Olympus high, and step o'er space and time ;
May stride with seven-leagu'd boots, from shore to shore,
And, nobly by transgressing, charm you more.
Alas ! our Author dares not laugh at schools,
Plain sense confines his humbler Muse to rules.
Form'd on the classic scale his structures rise,
He shifts no scenes to dazzle and surprize.
In one poor garden's solitary grove,
Like the primæval pair, his lovers rove.
And in due time will each transaction pass,
—— Unless some hasty critic shakes the glass.

PROLOGUE,

As it is spoken by Mr. GARRICK.

SUCCESS makes people vain.—The maxim's true;--
We all confess it — and not over new.
The veriest clown, who stumps along the streets,
And doffs his hat to each grave cit he meets,
Some twelvemonths hence, bedaub'd with livery lace,
Shall thrust his saucy flambeau in your face:

Not so our Bard—though twice your kind applause
Has, on this fickle spot, espous'd his cause :
He owns, with gratitude, th' obliging debt ;
Has twice been favour'd, and is modest yet.

Your giant wits, like those of old, may climb
Olympus high, and step o'er space and time ;
May stride, with seven-leagu'd boots, from shore to
shore,
And, nobly by transgressing, charm ye more.
Alas! our Author dares not laugh at schools ——
Plain sense confines his humbler Muse to rules :
He shifts no scenes—But here I stop'd him short ——
Not change your scenes? said I,—I'm sorry for't !
My constant friends above, around, below,
Have English tastes, and love both change and show :
Without such aids, even Shakespear would be flat——
Our crouded Pantomimes are proofs of that.
What eager transport stares from every eye,
When pullies rattle, and our Genii fly !

I,   *When*

PROLOGUE,

When tin cascades like falling waters gleam :
Or through the canvas—bursts the real stream :
While thirsty Islington laments in vain
Half her New-River roll'd to Drury-Lane.

Lord, Sir, said I, for gallery, boxes, pit, _
I'll back-my-Harlequin against your wit ——
Yet still the Author, anxious for his play,
Shook his wise head —— What will the critics say ?
As usual, Sir—abuse you all they can !—
And what the ladies —— He's a charming man !
A charming piece !—One scarce knows what it means ;
But that's no matter —— where there's such sweet
  scenes !
Still he persists—and let him—entre nous—
I know your tastes, and will indulge 'em too.
Change you shall have ; so set your hearts at ease :
Write as he will, we'll act it as you please.

PERSONS

Persons Reprefented.

Sir JOHN DORILANT, a Man of nice Honour, Guardian to Cælia, } Mr. GARRICK.

MODELY, BELMOUR, } Men of the Town, { Mr. PALMER. Mr. OBRIEN,

An old Steward to Sir John Dorilant, Mr. CASTLE.

Footman to Sir John Dorilant, Mr. FOX.

Lady BEVERLEY, a Widow Lady, Mother to Cælia, } Mrs. CLIVE.

CÆLIA, Daughter to Lady Beverley, and Ward to Sir John, } Mrs. CIBBER.

ARAMINTA, Sifter to Sir John Dorilant, } Mrs. YATES,

SCENE a Garden belonging to Sir John Dorilant's Houfe in the Country, with an Arbour, Garden Chairs, &c.

THE

School for LOVERS.

++

A C T   I.

SCENE *the Garden.*

Enter ARAMINTA *with an affected Careless-*
ness, and knotting, MODELY *following.*

MODELY.

BUT madam!

ARAMINTA.

But Sir! what can possibly have alarmed you
thus? You see me quite unconcerned. I only tell
you in a plain simple narrative manner —— (this
plaguy thread)—— and merely by way of conversation, that you are in love with Cælia; and where is
the mighty harm in all this?

MODELY.

The harm in it, madam! have I not told you a

thoufand and a thoufand times that you were the only woman who could poffibly make me happy?'

ARAMINTA.

Why aye, to be fure you have, and fworn a thoufand and a thoufand oaths to confirm that affertion.

MODELY.

And am not I here now exprefsly to marry you?

ARAMINTA.

Why that *too* is true ——— but ——— you are in love with Cælia.

MODELY.

Blefs me, madam, what can I fay to you? If it had not been for my attendance upon you, I had never known Cælia or her mother either, though they are both my relations. The mother has fince indeed put fome kind of confidence in me; fhe is a widow you know—

ARAMINTA.

And wants confolation! The poor orphan too her daughter! Well, charity is an excellent virtue. I never confidered it in that light before. You are vaftly charitable, Mr. Modely.

MODELY.

It is impoffible to talk with you. ——If you will not do me juftice, do it to yourfelf at leaft. Is there any comparifon betwixt you and Cælia? Could any man of fenfe hefitate a moment? She has yet no character. One does not know what fhe is, or what fhe will be; a chit, a green girl of fourteen or fifteen.

ARAMINTA.

Seventeen at lealt.—(I cannot undo this knot.)—

MODELY.

Well, let her be feventeen. Would any man of

judg-

judgment attach himself to a girl of that age? O'
my foul, if one was to make love to her, she
would hardly underſtand what one meant.

A R A M I N T A.

Girls are not quite ſo ignorant as you may imagine, Mr. Modely; Cælia will underſtand you,
take my word for it, and does underſtand you.
As to your men of judgment and ſenſe, here is my
brother now; I take him to be full as reaſonable as
yourſelf, and ſomewhat older; and yet with all
his philoſophy, he has brought himſelf to a determination at laſt, to fulfill the father's will, and
marry this green girl. I am ſorry to tell you ſo,
Mr. Modely, but he will certainly marry her.

M O D E L Y.

Let him marry her. I ſhould perhaps do it myſelf, if I was in his place. He was an intimate
friend of her father's. She is a great fortune, and
was given to him by will. But do you imagine,
my dear Araminta, that if he was left to his own
choice, without any bias, he would not rather
have a woman nearer his own years? He might almoſt be her father.

A R A M I N T A.

That is true. But you will find it difficult to
perſuade me, that youth in a woman is ſo inſur-
mountable an objection. I fancy, Mr. Modely, it
may be got over. Suppoſe I leave you to think of
it.—(I cannot get this right.)—— [*Going.*

M O D E L Y.

Stay, dear Araminta, why will you plague me
thus? Your own charms, my earneſtneſs, might
prove to you ——

A R A M I N T A.

I tell you I don't want proofs.

MODELY.

Well, well, you fhall have none then. But give me leave to hope, fince you have done me the honour to be a little uneafy on my account——

ARAMINTA.

Uneafy!——I uneafy!—— What does the man mean? I was a little concerned indeed to give you uneafinefs by informing you of my brother's intended marriage with Cælia. But——(this fhuttle bends fo abominably.)

MODELY.

Thou perplexing tyrant! Nay, you fhall not go.——May I continue to adore you! you muft not forbid me that.

ARAMINTA.

For my part I neither command nor forbid any thing. Only this I would have you remember, I have quick eyes. Your fervant.——(I wifh this knotting had never come in fafhion.)

[*Exit Araminta.*

MODELY.

Quick eyes indeed! I thought my cunning here had been a mafter-piece. The girl cannot have told fure! and the mother is entirely on my fide. They certainly were thofe inquifitive eyes fhe fpeaks of, which have found out this fecret. Well, I muft be more cautious for the future, and act the lover to Araminta ten times ftronger than ever. One would not give her up till one was fure of fucceeding in the other place.

Enter BELMOUR *from behind with a Book in his Hand.*

BELMOUR.

Ha! ha! ha! well faid Modely!

MODE-

MODELY (ſtarting.)

Belmour! how the duce came you here?

BELMOUR.

How came I here? —— How came you here—
if you come to that? A man can't retire from the
noiſe and buſtle of the world, to admire the beauties
of the ſpring, and read paſtoral in an arbour, but
impertinent lovers muſt diſturb his meditations.—
Thou art the erranteſt hypocrite, Modely ——

[*Throwing away the book.*

MODELY.

Hypocrite! —— My dear friend, we men of gallantry muſt be ſo. ——— But have a care, we may have
other liſteners for aught I know, who may not be
ſo proper for confidantes. [*Looking about.*

BELMOUR.

You may be eaſy on that head. We have
the garden to ourſelves. The widow and her
daughter are juſt gone in, and Sir John is buſy
with his ſteward.

MODELY.

The widow, and her daughter! Why, were they
in the garden?

BELMOUR.

They juſt came into it, but upon ſeeing you and
Araminta together, they turned back again.

MODELY.

On ſeeing me and Araminta? I hope I have no
jealouſies there too. However I am glad Cælia
knows I am in the garden, becauſe it may probably
induce her to fall in my way, by chance you know,
and give me an opportunity of talking to her.

BELMOUR.

Do you think ſhe likes you?

MODE-

MODELY.

She does not know what she does.

BELMOUR.

Do you like her?

MODELY.

Why faith, I think I do.

BELMOUR.

Why then do you pursue your affair with Araminta? and not find some honourable means of breaking off with her?

MODELY.

· That might not be quite so expedient. I think Araminta the finest woman, and Cælia the prettiest girl I know. Now they are both good fortunes, and one of them I am resolved to have, but which ————

BELMOUR.

Your great wisdom has not yet determined. Thou art undoubtedly the vainest fellow living—— I thought you brought me down here now to your wedding?

MODELY.

'Egad I thought so too, but this plaguy little rustic has disconcerted all my schemes. Sir John, you know, by her father's will, may marry her if he pleases, and she forfeits her estate if she marries any one else. Now I am contriving to bring it about, that I may get her, and her fortune too.

BELMOUR.

A very likely business, truly. So you modestly expect that Sir John Dorilant should give up his mistress, and then throw her fortune into the bargain, as an additional reward to the obliging man who has seduced her from him.

MODE-

MODELY.

Hum! why I don't expect quite that. But you know, Belmour, he is a man of honour, and would not force her inclinations tho' he loved her to diftraction. —— Come, come, he is quite a different creature from what you and I are.

BELMOUR.

Speak for yourfelf, good Sir; yet why fhould you imagine that her inclinations are not as likely to fix upon him as you? He has a good perfon, and is fcarce older than yourfelf.

MODELY.

That fhews your ignorance; I am ten years younger than he is. My drefs and the company I keep, give a youth and vivacity to me, which he muft always want. An't I a man of the town? O that town, Belmour! Could I but have met thefe ladies there, I had done the bufinefs.

BELMOUR.

Were they never there?

MODELY.

Never.——Sir Harry Beverley, the father of this girl, lived always in the country, and divided his time between his books and his hounds. His wife and daughter feldom mixed with people of their own rank, but at a horfe-race, or a rural vifit. And fee the effects! The girl, tho' fhe is naturally genteel, has an air of fimplicity.

BELMOUR.

But does not want fenfe.

MODELY.

No, no!—She has a devilifh deal of that kind of fenfe, which is acquired by early reading. I have heard her talk occafionally, like a queen in a tragedy, or at leaft like a fentimental lady in a comedy,

much

much above your miffes of thirty in town, I affure
you.——As to the mother——But fhe is a character, and explains herfelf.

BELMOUR.

Yes, yes, I have read her. But pray how came
it to pals, that the father, who was of a different
way of thinking in regard to party, fhould have left
Sir John guardian to his daughter, with the additional claufe too, of her being obliged to marry
him.

MODELY.

Why that is fomewhat furprizing. But the truth
of the cafe was, they were thoroughly acquainted,
and each confidered party as the foible of the other.
Sir Harry thought a good hufband his daughter's
beft fecurity for happinefs, and he knew it was impoffible Sir John Dorilant fhould prove a bad
one.

BELMOUR.

And yet this profpect of happinefs would you
deftroy.

MODELY.

No, no; I only fee farther than Sir Harry did,
and would increafe that happinefs, by giving her a
better hufband.

BELMOUR.

O! your humble fervant, Sir.

MODELY.

Befides, the mother is entirely in my intereft, and
by the by has a hankering after Sir John herfelf.
" He is a fober man, and fhould have a woman of
" difcretion for his wife, not a hoydening girl."—
'Egad, Belmour, fuppofe you attacked the widow?
The woman is young enough, and has an excellent
jointure.

BEL.

BELMOUR:

And fo became your father-in-law.

MODELY.

You will have an admirable opportunity to-night; we are to have the fiddles you know, and you may dance with her.

When mufick foftens, and when dancing fires! Eh! Belmour!

BELMOUR.

You are vaftly kind to Sir John, and would eafe him I find of both his miftreffes. But fuppofe this man of honour fhould be fool enough to refign his miftrefs, may not another kind of honour oblige him to run you through the body for deferting his fifter?

MODELY.

Why faith, it may. However, it is not the firft duel I have fought on fuch an occafion, fo I am his man. Not that it is impoffible but he may have fcruples there too.

BELMOUR.

You don't think him a coward?

MODELY.

I know he is not. But your reafoning men have ftrange diftinctions. They are quite different creatures, as I told you, from you and I.

BELMOUR.

You are pleafed to compliment. But fuppofe now, as irrational as you think me, I fhould find out a means to make this whole affair eafy to you?

MODELY.

How do you mean?

BELMOUR.

Not by attacking the widow, but by making my addreffes in good earneft to Araminta.

C   MODE-

MODELY.

I forbid that absolutely.

BELMOUR.

What, do you think it possible I should succeed after the accomplished Mr. Modely?

MODELY.

Why faith between you and I, I think not, but I don't chuse to hazard it.

BELMOUR.

Then you love her still?

MODELY.

I confess it.

BELMOUR.

And it is nothing upon earth but that insatiable vanity of yours, with a little tincture of avarice, that leads you a gadding thus?

MODELY.

I plead guilty. But be it as it will, I am determined to pursue my point. And see where the little rogue comes most opportunely. I told you she would be here. Go, go, Belmour, you must not listen to all my love scenes. [*Exit Belmour.* Now for a serious face, a little upon the tragic; young girls are mighty fond of despairing lovers.

Enter C Æ L I A.

C Æ L I A (with an affected surprize.)..

Mr. Modely!——are you here?——I am come to meet my mama—I did not think to find you here.

MODELY.

Are you sorry to find me here, madam?

C Æ L I A.

Why should I be sorry, Mr. Modely?

MODE-

MODELY.

May I hope you are pleaſed with it?

CÆLIA.

I have no diſlike to company.

MODELY.

But is all company alike? Surely one would chuſe one's companions. Would it have been the ſame thing to you, if you had met Sir John Dorilant here?

CÆLIA.

I ſhould be very ungrateful if I did not like Sir John Dorilant's company. I am ſure I have all the obligations in the world to him, and ſo had my poor papa, *(Sighing.*

MODELY.

Whatever were your papa's obligations, his gratitude I am ſure was unbounded.——O that I had been his friend!

CÆLIA.

Why ſhould you wiſh that, Mr. Modely?—— You would have had a great loſs in him.

MODELY.

I believe I ſhould. But I might likewiſe have had a conſolation for that loſs, which would have contained in it all earthly happineſs.

CÆLIA.

I don't underſtand you.

MODELY.

He might have left his Cælia to me.

CÆLIA.

Dear, how you talk!

MODELY.

Talk, madam!——O I could talk for ever, would you but liſten to my heart's ſoft language, nor cruelly affect to diſbelieve when I declare I love you.

C 2　　CÆLIA.

CÆLIA.

Love *me*, Mr. Modely?———Are not you in love with Araminta?

MODELY.

I once thought I was.

CÆLIA.

And do lovers ever change?

MODELY.

Not those who feel a real paffion. But there are falfe alarms in love, which the unpractifed heart fometimes miftakes for true ones.

CÆLIA.

And were yours fuch for Araminta?

MODELY.

Alas, I feel they were. *(Looking earneftly at her.)*

CÆLIA.

You don't intend to marry her then, I hope.

MODELY.

Do you hope I fhould not marry her?

CÆLIA.

To be fure I do. I would not have the poor lady deceived, and I would willingly have a better opinion of Mr. Modely than to believe him capahle of making faife proteftations.

MODELY.

To you he never could.

CÆLIA.

To me?——I am out of the queftion.——But I am forry for Araminta, for I believe fhe loves you.

MODELY.

If you can pity thofe who love in vain, why am not I an object of compaffion?

CÆLIA.

Dear Mr. Modely, why will you talk thus? My hand, you know, is deftined to Sir John Dorilant,

rilant, and my duty there does not even permit me to think of other lovers.

MODELY.

Happy, happy man ! Yet give me leave to afk one queftion, madam.——I dread to do it, tho' my laft glimpfe of happinefs depends upon your anfwer.

CÆLIA.

What queftion ?——Nay, pray fpeak, I intreat it of you.

MODELY.

Then tell me, lovely Cælia, fincerely tell me, were your choice left free, and did it depend upon you only to determine who fhould be the mafter of your affections, might I expect one favourable thought ?

CÆLIA (after fome hefitation.)

It—it does not depend upon me.

MODELY.

I know it does not, but if it did ?

CÆLIA.

Come, come, Mr. Modely, I cannot talk upon this fubject. Impoffibilities are impoffibilities.—— But I hope you will acquaint Araminta inftantly with this change in your inclinations.

MODELY.

I would do it, but I dare not.

CÆLIA.

You fhould break it firft to Sir John.

MODELY.

My difficulty does not lie in the breaking it; but if I confefs my paffion at an end, I muft no longer expect admittance into this family, and I could ftill wifh to talk to Cælia as a friend.

CÆLIA.

Indeed, Mr. Modely, I fhould be loth myfelf to Iofe your acquaintance; but —— O here comes my mama, fhe may put you in a method.

Enter

Enter LADY BEVERLEY.

LADY.

In any method, my dear, which decency and reserve will permit. Your servant, cousin Modely. What, you are talking strangely to this girl now?— O you men!

MODELY.

Your ladyship knows the sincerity of my passion here.

CÆLIA (with surprize.)

Knows your sincerity?

LADY.

Well, well, what signifies what I know?—You was mentioning some method I was to put you in.

CÆLIA.

Mr. Modely, madam, has been confessing to me that he no longer loves Araminta.

LADY.

Hum!—why such things may happen, child. We are not all able to govern our affections. But I hope if he breaks off with her, he will do it with decency.

MODELY.

That, madam, is the difficulty.

LADY.

What!——Is it a difficulty to be decent? Fie, fie, Mr. Modely.

MODELY.

Far be it from me even to think so, madam, before a person of your ladyship's reserved behaviour. But considering how far I have gone in the affair——

LADY.

Well, well, if that be all, I may perhaps help you out, and break it to Sir John myself.——Not that I approve of roving affections I assure you

MODE-

MODELY.

You bind me ever to you.——But there is another cauſe, which you alone can promote, and on which my eternal happineſs——

LADY.

Leave us—leave us, couſin Modely. I muſt not hear you talk in this extravagant manner.——[*Puſhing him towards the ſcene, and then aſide to him.*]——I ſhall bring it about better in your abſence, Go, go, man, go. [*Exit Modely.*]
A pretty kind of a fellow really.——Now Cælia, come nearer, child: I have ſomething of importance to ſay to you.——What do you think of that gentleman ?

CÆLIA.

Of Mr. Modely, madam ?

LADY.

Ay Mr. Modely, my couſin Modely.

CÆLIA.

Think of him, madam ?

LADY.

Ay, think of him, child ; you are old enough to think ſure after the education I have given you. Well, what anſwer do you make ?

CÆLIA.

I really don't underſtand your Ladyſhip's queſtion.

LADY.

Not underſtand me, child ? Why I aſk you how you like Mr. Modely ? What ſhould you think of him as a huſband.

CÆLIA.

Mr. Modely as a huſband ! Why ſurely madam, Sir John——

LADY.

LADY.

Fiddle faddle Sir John; Sir John knows better things than to plague himself with a wife in leading strings.

CÆLIA.

Is your ladyship sure of that?

LADY.

O ho! would you be glad to have me sure of it?

CÆLIA.

I don't know what I should be glad of. I would not give Sir John a moment's pain to be mistress of the whole world.

LADY.

But if it should be brought about without giving him pain. Hey! Cælia——[*Patting her cheek with her fan.*

CÆLIA.

I should be sorry for it.

LADY.

Hey day!

CÆLIA.

For then he must think lightly of me.

LADY.

What does the girl mean? Come, come, I must enter roundly into this affair. Here, here, sit down, and tell me plainly and honestly without equivocation or reservation, is Modely indifferent to you? Nay, nay,—look me in the face; turn your eyes towards me. One judges greatly by the eyes, especially in a woman. Your poor papa used to say that my eyes reasoned better than my tongue. —— Well, and now tell me without blushing, is Modely indifferent to you?

CÆLIA.

CÆLIA.

I fear he is not, madam, and it is that which perplexes me.

LADY.

How do you feel when you meet him?

CÆLIA.

Fluttered.

LADY.

Hum! ——While you are with him?

CÆLIA.

Fluttered.

LADY.

Hum! ——When you leave him?

CÆLIA.

Fluttered still.

LADY.

Strong symptoms truly!

CÆLIA.

When Sir John Dorilant talks to me, my heart is softened but not perplexed. My esteem, my gratitude overflows towards him. I consider him as a kinder father, with all the tenderness without the authority.

LADY.

But when Mr. Modely talks?

CÆLIA

My tranquility of mind is gone, I am pleased with hearing what I doubt is flattery, and when he grasps my hand ——

LADY,

Well, well, I know all that. ——Be decent, child. ——You need say no more, Mr. Modely is the man. *[Rising.*

D   CÆLIA.

CÆLIA.

But, dear Madam, there are a thoufand obftacles.
—I am afraid Sir John loves me; I am fure he
efteems me, and I would not forfeit his efteem for
the univerfe. I am certain I can make him an affectionate and an humble wife, and I think I can
forget Mr. Modely.

LADY.

Forget a fiddle! Don't talk to me of forgetting.
I order you on your duty not to forget. Mr.
Modely is, and fhall-be the man. You may truft
my prudence for bringing it about. I will talk
with Sir John inftantly.——I know what you are
going to fay, but I will not hear a word of it. Can
you imagine, Cælia, that I fhall do any thing but
with the utmoft decency and decorum ?

CÆLIA.

I know you will not, madam ; but there are delicacies ——

LADY.

With which I am unacquainted to be fure, and
my daughter muft inftruct me in them. Pray,
Cælia, where did you learn this nicety of fentiments?
Who was it that infpired them ?

CÆLIA.

But the maxims of the world ——

LADY.

Are altered, I fuppofe, fince I was of your age.
Poor thing, what world haft thou feen ? Notwithftanding your delicacies and your maxims, Sir John
perhaps may be wifer than you imagine, and chufe a
wife of fomewhat more experience.

CÆLIA.

May he be happy wherever he chufes.——But
dear madam ——

LADY.

LADY.

Again? don't make me angry. I will positively not be instructed. Ay, you may well blush.——
Nay, no tears——Come, come, Cælia, I forgive you. I had idle delicacies myself once. Lard! I remember when your poor papa —— he, he, he—— but we have no time for old stories. What would you say now if Sir John himself should propose it, and persuade the match, and yet continue as much your friend as ever, nay become more so, a nearer friend.

CÆLIA.

In such a case, madam ————

LADY.

I understand you, and will about it instantly. B'ye Cælia; O how its little heart flutters!

[*Exit Lady.*

CÆLIA.

It does indeed. A nearer friend? I hardly know whether I should wish her success or not—Sir John is so affectionate. Would I had never seen Mr. Modely!——Araminta too! what will she say?
—— O I see a thousand bad consequences. I must follow her, and prevent them.

END of the FIRST ACT.

ACT II.

SCENE *continues*.

LADY BEVERLEY *and* MODELY.

LADY.

PRITHEE don't teize me fo; I vow, coufin
Modely, you are almoft as peremptory as my
daughter. She truly was teaching me decorum
juft now, and plaguing me with her delicacies, and
her ftuff. I tell you Sir John will be in the garden immediately, this is always his hour of walking : and when he comes, I fhall lay the whole
affair before him, with all its concatenation of circumftances, and I warrant you bring it ahout.

MODELY.

I have no doubt, madam, of the tranfcendency
of your ladyfhip's rhetorick ; it is on that I entirely
rely. But I muft beg leave to hint, that Araminta
already fufpects my paffion, and fhould it be
openly declared, would undoubtedly prevail that
inftant with her brother to forbid me the houfe.

LADY.

Why, that might be.

MODELY.

And tho' I told your daughter I did not care
how foon it came to an eclaircifment, yet a woman
of your ladyfhip's penetration and knowledge of

the

the world, muſt ſee the neceſſity of concealing it, at leaſt for a time. I beg pardon for offering what may have even the diſtant appearance of inſtruction. But it is Sir John's delicacy which muſt be principally alarmed with apprehenſions of her diſregard for him ; and I am ſure your ladyſhip's manner of doing it, will ſhew him where he might much better place his affections, and with an undoubted proſpect of happineſs.

LADY.

Ay, now you talk to the purpoſe.--But ſtay, is not that Sir John coming this way ?—It is I vow, and Araminta with him. We'll turn down this walk, and reaſon the affair a little more, and then I will come round the garden upon him.

[*Modely takes her hand to lead her out.*
You are very gallant, couſin Modely. [*Exeunt.*

Enter SIR JOHN DORILANT and ARAMINTA.

ARAMINTA.

What do you drag me into the garden for ? We were private enough where we were——and I hate walking.

SIR JOHN.

Forgive me, my dear ſiſter ; I am reſtleſs every where, my head and heart are full of nothing but this lovely girl.

ARAMINTA.

My dear, dear brother, you are enough to ſpoil any woman in the univerſe. I tell you again and again, the girl is a good girl, an excellent girl, and will make an admirable wife. You may truſt one woman in her commendations of another ; we are

not

not apt to be too favourable in our judgments, especially when there is beauty in the case.

S I R J O H N.

You charm me when you talk thus. If she is really all this, how happy must the man be who can engage her affections. But alas! Araminta, in every thing which regards me, it is duty, not love, which actuates her behaviour. She steals away my very foul by her attentions, but never once expresses that heart-felt tendernes, those sympathetic feelings.

A R A M I N T A.

Ha—ha—ha!——O my stars!——Sympathetic feelings!—Why, would you have a girl of her age have those sympathetic feelings, as you call them! If she had, take my word for it, she would coquet it with half the fellows in town before she had been married a twelvemonth. Besides, Sir John, you don't consider that you was her father's friend; she has been accustomed from her infancy to respect you in that light; and our fathers friends, you know, are always old people, grey beards, philosophers, enemies to youth, and the destruction of gayety.

S I R J O H N.

But I was never such.

A R A M I N T A.

You may imagine so; but you always had a grave turn. I hated you once myself.

S I R J O H N.

Dear Araminta!

A R A M I N T A.

I did as I hope to live; for many a time has your aversion to dancing hindered me from having a fiddle.---By the by, remember we are to have the fiddles to night.—But let that pass: As the case now stands, if I was not already so near akin to you, you have the temper in the world which I should chuse in a husband.

SIR JOHN
That is obliging, however.

ARAMINTA.
Not so very obliging perhaps neither. It would be merely for my own sake, for then would I have the appearance of the most obedient sympathetic wife in the universe, and yet be as despotic in my government as an eastern monarch. And when I grew tired, as I probably should do, of a want of contradiction, why, I should find an easy remedy for that too—— I could break your heart in about a month.

SIR JOHN.
Don't trifle with me, 'tis your serious advice I want; give it me honestly as a friend, and tenderly as a sister.

ARAMINTA.
Why I have done it, fifty times. What can I say more? If you will have it again you must. This then it is in plain terms.—But you are sure you are heartily in love with her?

SIR JOHN.
Pshaw!

ARAMINTA.
Well then, that we will take for granted; and now you want to know what is right and proper for you to do in the case. Why, was I in your place, I should make but short work with it. She knows the circumstances of her father's will, therefore, would I go immediately to her, tell her how my heart flood inclined, and hope she had no objections to comply, with what it is not in her power to refuse.

SIR

SIR JOHN.

You would not have me talk thus abruptly to her ?

ARAMINTA.

Indeed I would. It will fave a world of trouble. She will blufh perhaps at firft, and look a little aukward, (and by the by fo will you too); but if fhe is the girl I take her for, after a little irrefolute gefture, and about five minutes converfation, fhe will drop you a curtefy with the demure humility of a Veftal, and tell you it fhall be as you and her mama pleafes.

SIR JOHN.

O that it were come to that !

ARAMINTA.

And pray what hinders it ? Nothing upon earth but your confummate prudence and difcretion.

SIR JOHN.

I cannot think of marrying her, till I am fure fhe loves me.

ARAMINTA.

Lud, Lud !—why what does that fignify ? If fhe confents is not that enough ?

SIR JOHN.

Her gratitude may induce her to confent, rather than make me unhappy.

ARAMINTA.

You would abfolutely make a woman mad.

SIR JOHN.

Why, could you think of marrying a man who had no regard for you.

ARAMINTA.

The cafe is widely different, my good cafuiftical brother ; and perhaps I could not —— unlefs I was very much in love with him.

SIR

SIR JOHN.

And could you then?

ARAMINTA.

Yes I could ——— to tell you the truth I believe
I shall.

SIR JOHN.

What do you mean?

ARAMINTA.

I shall not tell you.—You have business enough
of your own upon your hands.

SIR JOHN.

Have you any doubts of Modely?

ARAMINTA.

I shall keep them to myself if I have.   For you
are a wretched counsellor in a love case.

SIR JOHN.

But dear Araminta——

ARAMINTA.

But dear Sir John Dorilant, you may make yourself perfectly easy, for you shall positively know nothing of my affairs.   As to your own, if you do not
instantly resolve to speak to Cælia, I will go and
talk to her myself.

SIR JOHN.

Stay, lady Beverley is coming towards us.

ARAMINTA.

And has left my swain yonder by himself.

SIR JOHN.

Suppose I break it to her?

ARAMINTA.

It is not a method which I should advise; but do
as you please.—— I know that horrid woman's sen-
timents very exactly, and I shall be glad to have
her teized a little (*Aside.*) ——— I'll give you an op-
E   portunity

portunity by leaving you; and so adieu, my dear
sentimental brother!

We'll change partners if you please, madam — [*To
lady Beverley as she enters.* —*And then exit to*
[*Modely.*

LADY BEVERLEY.

Poor mistaken creature! how fond the thing is!--
[*Aside, and looking after Araminta.*
Your servant, Sir John.

SIR JOHN.

Your ladyship's most obedient. —— [*After some
irresolute gesture on both sides* —— *lady Beverley
speaks.*]

LADY.

I-- I--- have wanted an opportunity of speaking
to you, Sir John, a great while.

SIR JOHN.

And I, madam, have long had an affair of consequence to propose to your ladyship.

LADY.

An affair of consequence to me! —— O Lud—
you will please to speak, Sir.

SIR JOHN

Not till I have heard your ladyship's commands.

LADY.

What, must women speak first? Fie, Sir John ——
(*looking languishingly*) —— Well then, the matter in
short is this, I have been long thinking how to dispose of my girl properly. She is grown a woman
you see, and tho' I who am her mother say it, has
her allurements.

SIR JOHN.

Uncommon ones indeed.

LADY.

LADY.

Now I would willingly confult with you how to
get her well married, before fhe is tainted with the
indecorums of the world.

SIR JOHN.

It was the very fubject which I propofed fpeak-
ing to you upon.—— I am forry to put your ladyfhip in mind of a near and dear lofs—But you remember Sir Harry's will.

LADY.

Yes, yes, I remember it very well.   Poor man!
it was undoubtedly the only weak thing he was
ever guilty of.

SIR JOHN.

Madam!

LADY.

I fay, Sir, John we muft pardon the failings of
our deceafed friends.   Indeed his affection for his
child excufes it.

SIR JOHN.

Excufes it!

LADY.

Yes indeed does it.   His fondnefs for her might
naturally make him wifh to place her with a perfon
of your known excellence of character ; for my own
part, had I died, I fhould have wifhed it myfelf.—I
don't believe you have your equal in the world.—
Nay, dear Sir John, 'tis no compliment.—This I fay
might make him not attend to the impropriety of
the thing, and the reluctance a gentleman of your
good fenfe and judgment muft undoubtedly have
to accede to fo unfuitable a treaty.   Efpecially as
he could not but know there were women of difcretion in the world, who would be proud of an al-
liance where the profpect of felicity was fo inviting
and unqueftionable.

E 2

SIR

SIR JOHN, (who had appeared uneasy all the time
      she was speaking.

What women, madam? I know of none.

L A D Y.

Sir John!—That is not quite so complaisant methinks —— to our sex, I mean.

S I R J O H N.

I beg your pardon, madam; I hardly know what
I say. Your ladyship has disconcerted every thing
I was going to propose to you.

L A D Y.

Bless me, Sir John!—I disconcerted every thing?
How pray? I have been only talking to you in an
open friendly manner, with regard to my daughter,
our daughter indeed I might call her, for you have
been a father to her. The girl herself always
speaks of you as such.

S I R J O H N.

Speaks of me as a father?

L A D Y.

Why, more unlikely things have happened, Sir
John.

S I R J O H N.

Than what, madam?

L A D Y.

Dear Sir John!—You put such peremptory ques-
tions, you might easily understand what one meant
methinks.

S I R J O H N.

I find, madam, I must speak plain at once.——
Know then, my heart, my soul, my every thought
of happiness is fixed upon that lovely girl.

L A D Y.

O astonishing! Well, miracles are not ceased, that's
certain. But every body, they say, must do a foolish
             - thing

thing once in their lives.——And can you really
and ſeriouſly think of putting Sir Harry's will in
execution ?

SIR JOHN,

Would I could !

LADY.

To be ſure the girl has a fine fortune.

SIR JOHN.

Fortune! I deſpiſe it. I would give it with all
my ſoul to any one who could engage me her affections.——Fortune ! dirt.

LADY.

I am thunderſtruck !————

SIR JOHN. (Turning eagerly to her.)

O madam, tell me, ſincerely tell me, what method can I poſſibly purſue to make her think fa-
vourably of me! You know her inmoſt ſoul, you
know the tender moments of addreſs, the eaſy
avenues to her unpractiſed heart. Be kind, and
point them out. [Graſping her hand.

LADY.

I vow, Sir John, I don't know what to ſay to
you. —— Let go my hand. —— You talked of
my diſconceiting you juſt now, I am ſure you diſ-
concert me with a witneſs.————(Aſide.) I did
not think the man had ſo much rapture in him.
He ſqueezed my hand with ſuch an emphaſis ! I
may gain him perhaps at laſt.

SIR JOHN.

Why will you not ſpeak, madam ? Can you ſee
me on the brink of deſperation, and not lend a friendly hand to my aſſiſtance ?

LADY.

I have it.—— (Aſide.)——Alas, Sir John, what
ſignifies

fignifies what I can do! Can I anfwer for the inclinations of a giddy girl?

SIR JOHN.

· You know fhe is not fuch; her innocent mind
is yet untainted with the follies of her fex. And if
a life devoted to her fervice, without a wifh but
what regards her happinefs, can win her to be
mine ————

LADY.

Why that might go a great way with an unpre-
judiced mind. But when a firft paffion has taken
place.

SIR JOHN. (With amazement.)
What do you mean?

LADY.

To tell you the truth, I am afraid the girl is
not fo untainted as you imagine.

SIR JOHN.

You diftract me.—— How——when ——whom
' can fhe have feen?

LADY.

Undoubtedly there is a man.

SIR JOHN.

Tell me who, that I may ——No, that I may
give her to him, and make her happy whatever becomes of me.

LADY.

That is generous indeed.——So——fo. [*Afide.*

SIR JOHN.

But 'tis impoffible. I have obferved all her mo-
tions, all her attentions, with a lover's eye incapa-
ble of erring.—Yet ftay—has any body written to
her?

LADY.

There are no occafion for letters, when people
are in the fame houfe together.

SIR

SIR JOHN.

Confufion !

LADY.

I was going to offer fome propofals to you, but your ftrange declaration flopped me fhort.

SIR JOHN.

You propofals ? —— You?—— Are you her abetter in the affair? —— O madam, what unpardonable crime have I committed againft you, that you fhould thus confpire my ruin ? Have not I always behaved to you like a friend, a brother ?—— I will not call you ungrateful.

LADY.

Mercy on us ! ——The man raves.— How could it poffibly enter into my head, or the girl's either, that you had any ferious thoughts of marrying her ? But I fee you are too much difcompofed at prefent, to admit of calm reafoning. So I fhall take fome other opportunity.——Friend——Brother —— Ungrateful !—Marry come up !—I hope, at leaft, you will not think of forcing the poor girl's inclinations ! Ungrateful indeed! [*Exit in a paffion.*

SIR JOHN.

Not for the univerfe.——Stay, madam.——She is gone.——But it is no matter. I am but little difpofed for altercation now. Heigh ho ! ——Good heaven ! can fo flight an intercourfe have effected all this ? — I have fcarce ever feen them together. O that I had been born with Belmour's happy talents of addrefs.—— Addrefs !——'tis abfolute . magick, 'tis fafcination — Alas! 'tis the rapidity of real paffion. —— Why did Modely bring him hither to his wedding ? Every thing has confpired againft me. He brought him, and the delay of the lawyers has kept him here. Had I taken Araminta's advice a poor fortnight ago, it had not been in the power of fate to have undone me. — And yet fhe might have

have feen him afterwards, which would at leaft have
made her duty uneafy to her.——Heigh ho!

Enter ARAMINTA *and* MODELY.

ARAMINTA. (Entering.)
I tell you, I heard them very loud! and I will fee
what is the matter. O! here is my brother alone.

SIR JOHN. (Taking her tenderly by the hand.)
O Araminta!——I am loft beyond redemption.

ARAMINTA.
Dear brother, what can have happened to you?

SIR JOHN. (Turning to Modely.)
Mr. Modely, you could not intend it, but you
have ruined me.

MODELY. (Alarmed.)
I, Sir John!

SIR JOHN.
You have brought a friend with you, who has
pierced me to the very foul.

MODELY.
Belmour!

SIR JOHN.
He has ftolen my Cælia's affections from me.

ARAMINTA. (Looking flyly at Modely.)
Belmour!

MODELY.
This muft he a miftake, but I'll humour it.
(*Afide.*) It cannot be, who can have told you fo?

SIR JOHN.
Her mother has been this inftant with me, to
make propofals on the fubject.

MODELY.
For Belmour!

SIR JOHN.
She did not abfolutely mention his name, but I
could

could not mistake it, For she told me the favoured
lover was under the same roof with us.

MODELY. (A little disconcerted:)
I could not have believed it of him.

ARAMINTA.
Nor do I yet.— [*Looking slyly again at Modely.*

MODELY.
There must certainly be some mistake in it; at
the worst, I am sure I can prevail so far with Belmour, as to make him drop his pretensions.

SIR JOHN.
You cannot make her ceafe to love him. [*Sighing.*

MODELY.
Time may easily get the better of so young a
passion.

SIR JOHN.
Never, never; she is too sincere, too delicately
senfible.

MODELY.
Come, come, you must not think so; it is not yet
gone so far, but that it may be totally forgotten.—
Now for a master-stroke to clench the whole——
(*Aside.*) In the mean time, Sir John, I have the
satisfaction of acquainting you, that my affair, with
Araminta's leave, draws very near a conclufion.
The lawyers have finished their papers, and I only
now wait for your perufal of them.

ARAMINTA. (Aside.)
Well said !

MODELY.
I ordered the writings to be laid upon your table.

ARAMINTA. (Aside.)
What does he mean ?

SIR JOHN.
Dear Mr. Modely, you shall not wait a moment
for me. I will difpatch them instantly. I feel the

F   wan:

want of happiness too severely myself, to postpone it
in others. I leave you with my sister ; when she
names the day, you may depend upon my concurrence.   *[Exit Sir John.*

(MODELY and ARAMINTA look at one another for some time, then he speaks.)

I hope, madam, you are now convinced of my
sincerity.

ARAMINTA.
I am absolutely struck dumb with your assurance.
MODELY. (With an affected surprize.)
Madam !

ARAMINTA.
You cannot mean all this.

MODELY.
Why not, madam ?

ARAMINTA.
Why, don't you know that I know——

MODELY.
I cannot help a lady's knowledge or imagina-
tions. All I know is, that it is in your power to
make me either the happiest or most miserable man
in the whole creation.

ARAMINTA.
Well, this is astonishing.

MODELY.
I am sorry, madam, that any unguarded behaviour of mine, any little playful gallantries, should
have occasioned surmises, which——

ARAMINTA.
Serious, as I hope to live.

MODELY.
Is it not enough to make one serious, when the
woman one has pursued for years, almost with adoration, is induced by mere appearances to doubt
                                                    the

the honourablenefs of one's intentions. Have you
not heard me this moment apply to your brother,
even in the midft of his uneafinefs.——I little expected where the difficulty would lie.

ARAMINTA.

Well, well, poor thing, I won't teize it any longer; here, there, take my hand.

MODELY.

Duped by Jupiter.——(*Afide.*)——O my ever-
lafting treafure! And when, and when fhall I be
happy?

ARAMINTA.

It fhall depend upon yourfelf.

MODELY.

To-morrow, then, my angel, be the day. O
Araminta, I cannot fpeak my tranfport.——And
did you really think that I was in love with Cælia?

ARAMINTA.

Why, as a proof of my future fincerity, I muft
confefs I did.

MODELY.

I wonder how you could.

ARAMINTA.

Come, come, there were grounds enough for a
woman in love to go upon.

MODELY. (taking her by the hand.)
But you are now perfectly eafy?

ARAMINTA. (pulling her hand from him.)
Why, yes, I think I am.——— But what can
my brother mean about Belmour?

MODELY.

It is fome trick of the widow's.

ARAMINTA.

I dare fay fhe meant you.

MODE-

MODELY.

Possibly she might ; you know her motives.

ARAMINTA.

Yes, yes, her passion for my brother is pretty no-
torious. But the wretch will be mistaken.——To-
morrow, you say ?

MODELY.

To-morrow, my adorable.

ARAMINTA.

It shall be as you please.——But my situation is
so terribly aukward, that I must break from you.
Adieu !   [*Exit Araminta.*

MODELY.

Upon my soul she is a fine woman ; and loves
me to distraction; and what is still more, I most undoubtedly love her.——I have a good mind to
take her.——Yet not to have it in my power to succeed in the other place, would call my parts in
question.——No, no; — I must not disparage my
parts neither.——In order to be a great character,
one should go as near being a rogue as possible. I
have a philosopher's opinion on my side in that,
and the practice of half the heroes and politicians
in Europe.

END of the SECOND ACT.

ACT III.

SCENE continues.

BELMOUR (alone.)

CÆLIA in love with me! Egad the thing is not impoſſible; my friend Modely may have been a little miſtaken. Sir John was very ſerious when he told me of it; and though I proteſted to him that I had never made the leaſt advances, he ſtill perſiſted in his opinion.—The girl muſt have have told him ſo herſelf.—Let me recollect a little. —— She is always extremely civil to me; but that indeed ſhe is to every body.—I do not remember any thing particular in her looks; but I ſhall watch them more narrowly the next time I ſee her.—She is very handſome; and yet in my opinion, notwithſtanding Modely's infidelity, Araminta is much the finer woman.—Suppoſe—— No, that will not do.

Enter MODELY.

MODELY.

So, ſo, Mr. Belmour, I imagined I ſhould find you here; this is the lover's corner. We have all had our reveries in it. But why don't you talk louder, man? You ought, at leaſt, to give me my revenge in that. My ſoliloquies, you know, are eaſily over-heard.

BEL-

BELMOUR.

I never defignedly over-heard them, Mr. Modely; nor did I make any improper ufe of the accident.

MODELY.

Grave, very grave, and perfectly moral! And fo this is all I am to have for the lofs of my miftrefs. —— Heigh ho!

Then I muft be content to fee her blefs
Yon happier youth.——

BELMOUR.

Your raillery is a little unfeafonable, Mr. Modely; for to fpeak plainly, I begin to fufpect that this is fome trick of yours, to dupe me as well as Sir John Dorilant.

MODELY.

Upon my honour, no, if we muft be ferious: it may be a miftake, but not intended on my fide, I can affure you. Come, come, if the girl really likes you, take her. If I fhould prove the happy man, give me joy, and there's an end of it.

BELMOUR.

I fancy you are ufed to difappointments in love, they fit fo eafy upon you. Or rather I fhould fuppofe, in this cafe, you are pretty fure of your ground.

MODELY.

Neither, upon my foul; but a certain *Je ne fçai quoy*, a *Gayete de Coeur* which carries me above misfortunes: fome people call it vanity.

BELMOUR.

And are not abfolutely miftaken. But what becomes of Araminta all this while?

MODELY. (yawning.)

I fhall marry her, I believe, to-morrow.

B E L-

BELMOUR.

Marry her?

MODELY.

Yes, Sir John is at this very moment looking
over the settlements.

BELMOUR.

I don't understand you.

MODELY.

And yet it is pretty plain, methinks. I tell
you I am to be married to-morrow. Was it not
time to make sure of one mistress, when you was
running away with the other?

BELMOUR.

You know I have no such intentions.———But
are you really serious? Have you laid aside your
designs upon Cælia?

MODELY.

Not so, neither.

BELMOUR.

What do you mean then by your marriage with
Araminta? Why won't you unriddle this affair to
me?

MODELY.

Because it is at present a riddle to myself, and I
expect lady Beverley here every moment to resolve
the enigma.

BELMOUR.

Was it a scheme of her's?

MODLEY.

Certainly, and I partly guess it, but will not un-
bosom till I know it fully.——Come, come, with all
that gravity of countenance and curiosity, you must
leave me instantly; the lady will be here, and the
plot unravelled, and then ------

BEL-

BELMOUR.

I fhall expect to be fatisfied. [*Exit.*

MODELY.

Ha! ha! ha! or elfe 'you fight me, I fuppofe. Why, fo you may; and fo may Sir John Dorilant too, and faith with fome colour of reafon. 'But my comfort is, that I have experience on my fide, and if I furvive the rencounter, I fhall be a greater hero than ever amongft the ladies, and be efteemed in all companies as much a man of honour as the beft of you.

Enter LADY BEVERLEY.

LADY.

Dear coufin Modely, I am all over in an agitation; we fhall certainly be difcovered; that devil Araminta ——

MODELY.

What of her, madam?

LADY.

Is now with her brother talking fo eagerly —— Oh! I faw the villainous changes in her countenance; I would have given the world to have overheard their converfation.—Come, come, you muft advife me inftantly.

MODELY.

Your ladyfhip muft firft let me into the fecret. I am abfolutely in a wood with regard to the whole affair. What is all this of Cælia and Belmour?

LADY.

Nothing, nothing at all; an errant dilemma of the foolifh man's own making, which his impertinent fifter will immediately clear up to him, and then all muft out.

MODE-

MODELY.

But how came Belmour ever to be mentioned in the cafe?

LADY.

Dear, dear, he never was mentioned. I muſt confeſs that I was ſo provoked with Sir John's unnatural behaviour, that I could not help telling him that Cælia had a lover, and in the houſe too. Your ſituation with regard to Araminta made him never dream of you, and confequently all his ſuſpicions turned on Belmour.

MODELY.

But you did not ſay that that lover had made his addreſſes to Cælia?

LADY.

I don't know what I might ſay; for he uſed me like a Turk. But whatever I ſaid I can unſay it again.

MODELY.

Why, if I might venture to advice a perſon of your lady's ſagacity! —— •

LADY.

O ay, with all my heart, couſin Modely. For though I may ſay it without vanity, that nobody has a more clear apprehenſion of things when the mental faculty is totally undiſturbed; yet, when I am in a trepidation, nobody upon earth can be more glad of advice.

MODELY.

Why, then, madam, to ſpeak with reverence, I ſhould hope your ladyſhip would ſee the neceſſity of keeping me as concealed as poſſible. It is the young lady's paſſion, not mine, which muſt have the principal influence. Sir John Doilant's peculiarity of temper is ſuch ————

G   LADY.

LADY.

Yes, yes, he has peculiarity enough, that's certain.

MODELY.

And it is there, madam, as the weakeſt part, that our attack will be the ſureſt. If ſhe confeſſes, an inclination for me, not both the Indies, added to her fortune, could induce him to marry her.

LADY.

That is honourable, however, couſin Modely. But he is a horrid creature, notwithſtanding.

MODELY.

I grant it, madam ; but a failure in an improper purſuit may recal his reaſon, and, as he does not want underſtanding, teach him to ſearch for happineſs where only it is to be expected.

LADY.

He! he! I am ſo angry with him at preſent, that I really believe I ſhould refuſe him.

MODELY.

Your ladyſhip muſt not be too cruel.

LADY.

Why, I confeſs it is not in my nature ; but— bleſs me, here they come. ———Let us run down this walk directly, for they muſt not ſee us together. [*Exeunt.*

Enter A R A M I N T A *and* S I R J O H N
D O R I L A N T.

A R A M I N T A.

Come along, I ſay, you dragged me into the garden juſt now, and I will command in my turn. Talk to her, you muſt and ſhall. The girl has ſenſe and ſpirit when ſhe is diſengaged from that

horrid

horrid mother of her's; and I have told her you wanted her, and in this very spot.

SIR JOHN.

You cannot feel, Araminta, what you make me suffer. But sooner or later it must come to this, and therefore I will assume a resolution, and be rid of all my doubts at once.

ARAMINTA.

I tell you, this nonsense about Belmour is merely a phantom of her mother's railing, to sound your intentions, and promote her own.

SIR JOHN.

Thus far is certain, that Belmour disclaims all knowledge of the affair, and with an appearance of sincerity; but even that is doubtful. Besides, they are not his, but her inclinations which give me any concern. It is the heart I require. The life-less form, beauteous as it is, would only elude my grasp; the shadow of a joy, not the reality.

ARAMINTA.

Dear, dear, that men had but a little common sense; or that one could venture to tell them what one knows of one's own sex! I have a good mind to be honest.———— As I live, the girl is coming. ——I'll speed her on the way. Courage, brother, Voila!   [*Exit.*

SIR JOHN.

How shall I begin with her?——What ideots are men when they have a real passion! ridiculous, beneath contempt. ———— [*Walks about the stage*] ——Suppose ———— I will not suppose; the honest heart shall speak its faithful dictates, and if it fails, ———— why, let it.

Enter C Æ L I A.

C Æ L I A (with timidity.)

Araminta tells me, Sir, that you had something to say to me.

SIR JOHN.

I have, madam. ——Come forward, Miss Beverley. ——Would you chuse to sit. —— [*They sit down.*] —— [*After some irresolute gesture.*] You are not afraid of catching cold?

C Æ L I A.

Not in the least, Sir.

SIR JOHN.

I know sitting in the open air has that effect upon some people ——but your constitution is yet untainted. ——Did my sister say any thing concerning the subject I would speak to you upon?

C Æ L I A.

She only told me, Sir, that it was of moment.

SIR JOHN.

It is of moment, indeed, Cælia. —— But you must not think that I am angry.

C Æ L I A.

Angry, Sir!

SIR JOHN.

I don't mean angry. —— I am a little confused; but I shall recover myself presently. ——[*Rises, and Cælia rises too.*] ——Nay, pray sit, Miss Beverley. ——Whatever I feel myself, I would not disturb you. ——[*Returns to his seat, then after a pause, goes on.*]——The affair I would speak to you upon is this: ——You remember your father perfectly?

C Æ L I A.

And ever shall.

SIR JOHN.

Indeed he was a good man, Miſs Beverley, a virtuous man, and felt tenderly for your happineſs. ——Thoſe tears become you, and yet, methinks, I would not provoke them. ——When he died, he left you to my care.

CÆLIA.

Which alone made his loſs ſupportable.

SIR JOHN.

Are you ſincere in what you ſay?

CÆLIA.

I ſhould be ungrateful indeed, if I was not.

SIR JOHN (turning towards her.)

Nay, you are ſincerity itſelf. – O Cælia [*Taking her by the band.*] ——But I beg your pardon, I am aſſuming a liberty I have no right to take, till you allow it.

CÆLIA.

Sir!

SIR JOHN.

I ſee I have alarmed you. ——Retire Miſs Beverley. ——I'll ſpeak to you ſome other time.—— [*She is going.*] —— Cælia, Miſs Beverley, —— pray come back, my dear. —— I am afraid my behaviour is rather too abrupt. —— Perhaps, too, it may diſpleaſe you.

CÆLIA.

I can be diſpleaſed with nothing from you, Sir; and am ready to obey you, be your commands what they will.

SIR JOHN.

Command, Cælia! ——that's a hard word.

CÆLIA.

I am ſorry it offends you.

SIR

3

SIR JOHN.

You know beft, Cælia, whether it ought to offend me; would I could read the fentiments of your heart! Mine are but too apparent.——In fhort, my dear, you know the purport of your father's will, dare you fulfil it?

CÆLIA.

To the minuteft circumftance.—— It is my duty.

SIR JOHN.

Ah, Cælia, that word *duty* deftroys the obligation.

CÆLIA.

Sir!——

SIR JOHN.

I don't know how it is, but I am afraid to afk you the only queftion, which fincerely anfwered, could make me happy—or miferable.   [*Half afide.*

CÆLIA.

Let me beg of you, fir, to afk it freely.

SIR JOHN.

Well then —— is your heart your own? O Cælia, that hefitation confirms my tears. You cannot anfwer in the affirmative, and have too much humanity for what I feel, to add to my torments. —Good God! — and is it poffible, that an acquaintance of a few days, fhould entirely obliterate the attentive affiduity, the tender anxieties which I have fhewn for years!--But I underftand it all too well. Mine were the aweful, though heart-felt attentions of a parent; his, the fprightly addrefs of a prefuming lover. His eafy affurance has won upon your affections, and what I thought *my* greateft merit, has undone me.

CÆLIA.

You were fo good, fir, a little while ago, to pity
my

my confusion; pity it now, and whilst I lay my heart open before you, be again that kind, that generous friend, which I have always found you.

SIR JOHN.

Go on.——

CÆLIA.

It is in vain for me to dissemble an ignorance of your meaning, nor would I if I could. I own I have been too much pleased with Mr. Modely's conversation.

SIR JOHN.

Modely's?

CÆLIA.

Let me go on.—— His intended marriage with Araminta, gave him a freedom in the family which it was not my business to restrain. His attentions to my mother, and the friendly manner in which he executed some commissions of consequence to her, gave him frequent opportunities of talking to me. I will confess too, that his appearance and his manner struck me. But I was so convinced of his real passion for Araminta, that I never dreamt of the least attachment to me, till——

SIR JOHN.

Till what, when— Modely?——Why, he is to be married to my sister to-morrow or next day.

CÆLIA.

I know it was so intended, but his behaviour this morning, and the intercessions of my mother, had, I own, won upon me strongly, and induced me to believe that I only was the object of his pursuits.

SIR JOHN.

I am thunderstruck!——

CÆLIA.

My mother made me clearly perceive that the
com-

completion of his marriage would be an injury to Araminta.   She told me too, fir, that you yourfelt would be my advifer in the affair, and even perfuaded me to accept it.

SIR JOHN.

O the malicious woman !

CÆLIA.

In that indeed I perceive fhe greatly erred.   And I only mean this as a confeffion of what is paft, and of what is now at an end for ever.——For the future, I give myfelf to your guidance alone, and am what you direct. ——   [*Giving her hand to him.*

SIR JOHN.

Thou amiable foftnefs !——No, Cælia, however miferable I may be myfelf, I will not make you fo ; it was your heart, not your hand I afpired to. As the former has been feduced from me, it would be an injuftice to us both to accept of the latter. As to Mr. Modely, and Lady Beverley, I have not deferved this treachery from them, and they fhall both feel my refentment.

CÆLIA.

Sir !

SIR JOHN.

She told me indeed there was a favoured lover, and my fufpicions fell very naturally upon Belmour. Nay, even now, nothing but that lovely fincerity— which undoes me—could make me credit this villainy of Modely. ——O Cælia ! what a heart have I loft !

CÆLIA.

You cannot, fhall not lofe it ; worthlefs as it is, 'tis yours, and only yours, my father, guardian, lover, hufband !   [*Hangs upon him weeping.*

Enter

Enter A R A M I N T A.

A R A M I N T A.

Hey day! what a fcene is here! What is the matter with ye both.

S I R J O H N.

O fifter! that angel goodnefs, that mirror of her fex, has ruined me.

A R A M I N T A.

Ruined you! how?

S I R J O H N.

Nay, I am not the only fufferer, Modely is as falfe to you, as her mother is to all of us.

A R A M I N T A.

I don't underftand you.

S I R J O H N.

You will too foon. My fufpicions of Belmour were all a chimæra; it is your impious Modely who has poffeffion of her heart.——To me fhe is loft irrecoverably.——   [*Going.*

A R A M I N T A.

Stay, brother.

S I R J O H N.

I cannot, my foul's too full.   [*Exit.*

A R A M I N T A.

Pray, mifs Beverley, what is the meaning of all this?

C Æ L I A.

I cannot fpeak——[*Throwing herfelf into a chair.*

A R A M I N T A.

I'll be hang'd if this fellow Modely has not talked you into an opinion, that he is in love with you; indeed, my dear, your youth and inexperience may lead you into ftrange fcrapes; and that mother of

H   yours

yours is enough to turn any girl's head in the univerſe. Come, come, unriddle this affair to me.

CÆLIA.

Alas! madam, all I know is, that the only man
I ever did, or ever can eſteem, deſpiſes me, and, I
fear, hates me.

ARAMINTA.

Hates you ! he doats upon you to diſtraction.——
But pray, did Modely ever make any ſerious addreſſes to you ?

CÆLIA.

Alas ! but too often.

ARAMINTA.

The hypocrite! but I'll be even with him. ——
And your mother, I ſuppoſe, encouraged him ? An
infamous woman ! But I know her drift well
enough.———

Enter LADY BEVERLEY.

LADY.

Where is my poor girl ? I met Sir John Dorilant in ſuch a furious way, that he ſeems to have
loſt all common civility. What have they done to
you, child ?

ARAMINTA.

Done to her ? What has your ladyſhip done
to her ? I knew your little artifices long ago,
but ———

LADY.

My artifices ! Mrs. Araminta.

ARAMINTA.

Your artifices, lady Beverley ; but they are all
to no purpoſe; the girl has too good an underſtanding to be impoſed upon any longer; and your boaſt-

ed

ed machinations are as vain and empty in their effect, as in their contrivance.

LADY.

What does the woman mean? But the loss of a lover, I suppose, is an excuse for ill-breeding! Poor creature! if the petulancy of thy temper would let me, I could almost pity thee. The loss of a lover is no agreeable thing; but women at our time of life, Mrs. Araminta, must not expect a lasting passion.

ARAMINTA.

Scarce any at all I believe, if they go a wooing themselves. For my part, I have had the satisfaction of being sollicited however. And I am afraid my rustic brother never gave your ladyship's sollicitations even the slightest encouragement. How was it? Did you find him quite hard-hearted? No bowels of compassion for so accomplished a damsel?

CÆLIA. (interposing.)

Dear madam! dear Araminta!

LADY.

Stand away, child. ——Desert, madam, is not always attended with success, nor confidence neither. There are some women so assured of their conquest, as even to disgust a lover on the very day of marriage.

ARAMINTA.

Was my behaviour ever such?

LADY.

I really cannot say, Mrs. Araminta; but the world, you know, is censorious enough, when a match is broken off so near its conclusion, as generally to charge the inconstancy of the lover on some defect in his mistress.

ARA-

ARAMINTA.

I defy him to produce any.

LADY.

And yet he has certainly left you ; " Never, ah " never to return."

ARAMINTA.

Infolent!

CÆLIA. (interpofing again.)

Dear Araminta!

ARAMINTA.

But your ladyfhip may be miftaken even in that too. I may find him at his follicitations again ; and if I do ———

LADY.

You'll take him.

ARAMINTA.

Take him ?———Daggers and poifon fooner.

LADY.

Poor creature!—Come, Cælia, words do but ag-gravate her misfortune. We only difturb her. You fee, my dear, what are the effects of too vio-lent a paffion. It may be a leffon for your future conduct.

ARAMINTA.

Look you, lady Beverley, don't provoke me,

LADY.

Why, what will you do?

CÆLIA. (interpofing.)

For heaven's fake, madam ———

LADY.

I fancy, Mrs. Araminta, inftead of quarrelling, we had better join forces. If we could but get this girl out of the way, we might both fucceed.

ARAMINTA.

You are a wicked woman, ———

LADY.

LADY.

Poor creature! shall I say any thing to my cousin Modely for you? You know I have weight with him.

ARAMINTA.

Yes, madam; you may tell him that his connections with you, have rendered him ridiculous; and that the revenge of an injured woman is never contemptible. [*Exit Araminta.*

LADY. (leading off Cælia on the other side.)

Poor creature!——Come along, child,

END of the THIRD ACT.

ACT IV.

SCENE *continues.*

SIR JOHN DORILANT, *alone.*

T HIS fatal spot, which draws me to it almost involuntarily, must be the scene of another interview.——Thank heaven I have recovered myself. Nor shall any misery which I may suffer, much less any prospect of a mean revenge, make me act unbecoming my character.

Enter ARAMINTA.

ARAMINTA.

Well, brother, I hope you are resolved to marry this girl.

SIR JOHN.

Marry her, my dear Araminta? Can you think it possible, that I should have so preposterous a thought? No, my behaviour shall deserve her, but not over-rule her inclinations. Were I to seize the tender opportunity of her present disposition, the world would ascribe it to her fortune; and I am sure my deceased and valuable friend, however kindly he meant to me in the affair, never intended that I should make his daughter unhappy.

ARA-

ARAMINTA.

But I tell you she loves you ; and you must and shall marry her.

SIR JOHN.

Ah sister, you are willing to dispose of her any way. That worthless lover of yours still hangs about your heart, and I have avoided seeing him on your account, as well as Cælia's.

ARAMINTA.

To shew how mistaken you are in all this, I have given him up totally. I despise, and hate him ; nay I am upon the brink of a resolution to give myself to another.   [*Sir John shakes his head.*
I am, I assure you ; his friend Mr. Belmour is by no means indifferent on my subject.

SIR JOHN.

And is this revenge on yourself, a proof of your want of passion for him ?—Ah Araminta!—Come, come, my dear, I own I think him unworthy of you, and would resent his usage to the utmost, did not I clearly perceive that it would appear mercenary in myself, and give real pain both to you and Cælia.

ARAMINTHA.

I actually don't know what to say to you.

SIR JOHN.

You had better say nothing. Your spirits at present are too much alarmed. —I have sent for Cælia hither, a short hour may determine the fates of all of us. I know my honourable intentions will give her great uneasiness. But it is my duty which exacts them from me.—You had better take a turn or two in some other part of the garden ;— I see my steward coming this way :—I may want your assistance but too soon.   [*Exit Araminta.*

Enter

Enter STEWARD.

Have you brought those papers I bad you look out?

STEWARD.
Yes, Sir. But there is the gentleman within to wait upon your honour, concerning the estate you intended to purchase. It seems a mighty good bargain.

SIR JOHN.
I cannot speak to him now.

STEWARD.
Your honour always used to be punctual.

SIR JOHN.
Alas! Jonathan, I may be punctual again to-morrow.—Give me the papers. Did Miss Beverley say she would come to me?

STEWARD.
Immediately, Sir. But I wish your honour would consider, such bargains as these do not offer every day.

SIR JOHN.
Heigh ho!

STEWARD.
It joins so conveniently too to your honour's own estate, within a hedge as I may say.

SIR JOHN.
Prithee don't plague me.

STEWARD.
Nay, 'tis not my interest, but your honour's. Tho' that indeed I may call my interest, for I am sure I love your honour.

SIR JOHN.
I know thou dost, Jonathan, and I am too hasty,

I   but

—but leave me now.—If the gentleman will do me the favour of staying all night, I may satisfy him in the morning. My head and heart are too full now for any businefs which concerns my fortune.

STEWARD.

Something goes very wrong with my poor mafter. Some love nonfenfe or other I fuppofe—— I wifh all the women were in the bottom of the fea, for my part. [*Exit Steward.*

Enter L A D Y B E V E R L E Y *and* C Æ L I A.

L A D Y.

I thought it requifite, Sir John, as I heard you had fomething of importance to tranfact with my daughter, to wait upon you with her.

SIR JOHN.

Was that neceffary, madam ?—I begged the favour of Mifs Beverley's company only.

L A D Y.

But a mother, you know, Sir John, who has a tender concern for her child ——

SIR JOHN.

Should fhew it upon every occafion.

L A D Y.

I find, Sir John, there is fome mifunderftanding at prefent, which a woman of prudence and experience might be much better confulted upon, than a poor young thing, whofe—— -

SIR JOHN.

Not at all, madam ; Cælia has all the prudence I require, and our prefent converfation will foon be over.

I LADY.

LADY.

Nay, Sir John, to be sure I am not afraid of trust-ing my daughter alone with you. A man of your discretion will undoubtedly be guilty of no impropriety. . But a third person sometimes, where the parties concerned are a little too much influenced by their passions, has occasioned very substantial, and very useful effects. I have known several in-stances of it, in the course of my experience.

SIR JOHN.

This, madam, will not be one of them.—How teizing!   ' [Walking aside.

LADY.

I find, Sir John, that you are determined to have your own way, and therefore I shall shew you by my behaviour, that I know what good manners re-quire, tho' I do not always meet with the same treatment from other people.   [Exit Lady.

SIR JOHN.

Now, Cælia, we are alone, and I have many excuses to make to you for the impassioned sallies of our late conversation ; which I do most sincere-ly.—Can you pardon them ?

CÆLIA.

Alas! Sir, 'tis I who ought to intreat for pardon.

SIR JOHN.

Not in the least, madam, I have no blame to cast upon you for any part of your conduct. Your youth and inexperience, joined to the goodness of your heart, are sufficient apologies for any shadow of indiscretion which might appear in your behavi-our. I am afraid mine was not so irreproachable. However, Cælia, I shall endeavour to make you all the amends in my power; and to shew you that it is your happiness, not my own, which is the object of my anxiety.

Your father's will is but too clear in its intentions. But the purity of his heart never meant to promote my felicity at the expence of yours. You are therefore, madam, entirely at liberty from this moment, to make your choice where you please. This paper will entitle you to that authority, and this will enable you to bestow your fortune where you bestow your hand.——Take them, my dear !

——Why are you so disturbed ?——Alas, Cælia, I see too plainly the cause of these emotions. You only wish the happy man to whom you have given your heart, loved you as I do ! ——

But I beg pardon ; and will only add one caution, which my duty demands of me, as your guardian, your protector, and your father's friend.——You have been a witness of Modely's transactions with my sister. Have a care therefore, Cælia ; be sure of his firm attachment before you let your own hurry you into a compliance. These papers give you up all power on my part ; but as an adviser, I shall be always ready to be consulted.

C Æ L I A.

My tears and my confusion have hitherto hindered me from answering ; not the invidious suggestion which you have so cruelly charged me with. What friend, what lover have I, to engross my attentions ? I never had but one, and he has cast me off for ever.——O, Sir, give me the papers, and let me return them where my soul longs to place them.

SIR JOHN.

No, Cælia, to accept them again, would impeach the justice of my whole proceeding. It

would make it look like the mean artifice of a mercenary villain, who attempted to gain by ſtratagem what his merits did not entitle him to.——I bluſh to think of it.—I have performed my office. Be miſtreſs of yourſelf, and let me fly from a combat to which I find myſelf unequal. [*Exit Sir John.*
(CÆLIA ſits down, leaning her head upon her hand.)

Enter MODELY *and* BELMOUR.
MODELY.
Hiſt! hiſt! he has juſt left her, and in a fine ſituation for my approaches.————If you are not yet ſatisfied, I will make up all differences with you another time.——Get into the arbour, and be a witneſs of my triumph. You ſhall ſee me, like another Cæſar, Come, See—and Overcome.
[*Belmour goes into the arbour.*
(MODELY comes forward, walks two or three turns by her, bowing as he paſſes, without being taken notice of, then ſpeaks.)
If it is not an interruption, madam, when I find you thus alone ——

CÆLIA (riſing.)
I would chuſe to be alone.
MODELY.
Madam!
CÆLIA (after a little pauſe.)
In ſhort, Mr. Modely, your behaviour to me of late is what I can by no means approve of. It is unbecoming your character as a man of honour, and would be a ſtain to the ingenuous modeſty of my ſex for me to ſuffer it.
MODELY.
You ſurprize me, madam. Can the adoration of an humble love, the timid advances of a man whom

whom you beauty has undone, be such unpardonable offences?

(CÆLIA looks with indignation at him, and is going off.)

MODELY (catching hold of her, and falling upon his knees.)
Nay, madam, you muſt not leave me!

CÆLIA.
Riſe, Sir, or I am gone this moment.————I thought of flying from you, but my ſoul diſdains it. ————Know then, Sir, that I am miſtreſs of myſelf, miſtreſs of my fortune, and may beſtow my hand wherever my heart directs it.

MODELY.
My angel!—— [Coming eagerly up to her.

CÆLIA.
What do you mean?

MODELY.
That you make the moſt ſincere of lovers, the happieſt of mankind. The addition of your fortune will add ſplendor to our felicity; and the frowns of diſappointed love, only heighten our enjoyments.

CÆLIA.
Oh thou vile one!——How does that cruel generous man who has rejected me, riſe on the compariſon!

MODELY.
Rejected you?——Sir John Dorilant?

CÆLIA.
Yes, Mr. Modely, that triumph at leaſt is yours. I have offered myſelf, and been refuſed. My hand and fortune equally diſdained. But may perpetual happineſs attend him, where'er his honeſt, honeſt heart ſhall fix!

MODE-

M O D E L Y.

O, madam, your inexperience deceives you.
He knows the integrity of your mind, and trusts
to that for recompence. His feeming difinterefted-
nefs is but the furer method of compleating his
utmoft wifhes.

C Æ L I A.

Blafphemer, ftop thy tongue. The purity of his
intentions is as much above thy malice, as thy imi-
tation.

[*She walks to one fide of the ftage, and Modely
ftands difconcerted on the other.*

Enter L A D Y   B E V E R L E Y.

L A D Y.

Well, child, what has the man faid to thee ?
Coufin Modely, your fervant; you find our plot
would not take, they were too quick upon us. ——
Hey day ! what has been doing here ?

M O D E L Y.

O, madam, you are my only refuge; a wretch
on the brink of defpair flies to you for protection.
That amiable creature is in full poffeffion of herfelf
and fortune, and yet rejects my tendereft follicitations.

L A D Y.

Really !——What is all this ? Tell me, Cælia,
has the man actually given up all right and title to
thee real and perfonal ? Come, come, I muft be a
principal actrefs, I find, in this affair.——Decency
and decorum require it.—Tell me, child, is it fo?

C Æ L I A.

Sir John Dorilant, madam, with a generofity
peculiar to himfelf, (cruel generofity !) has cancelled
every obligation which could confine my choice.
Thefe

Thefe papers confirm the freedom he has given me
——and rob me of all future comfort.

L A D Y.

Indeed ! I did not expect this of him ; but I am
heartily glad of it. Give *me* the papers, child.

C Æ L I A.

No, madam !——Ufelefs as they are, they are
yet my own.

L A D Y.

Ufelefs ?——What do you mean ? Has the bafe
man laid any other embargo on thee, child ?

C Æ L I A.

I cannot bear, madam, even from you, to hear
Sir John Dorilant treated with difrefpect.——
Ufelefs ! ——Yes, they fhall be ufelefs. Thus, thus
I tear them into atoms, and difdain a liberty which
but too juftly reproaches *my* conduct. Your advice, madam, has already made me miferable, but
it fhall not make me ungrateful or unjuft.

[Exit Cælia.

L A D Y.

I am aftonifhed, I never faw the girl in fuch a
way before. Why this is errant difobedience,
coufin Modely. I muft after her, and know the
bottom of it.—Don't defpair. *[Exit Lady.*

B E L M O U R (coming out of the arbour.)
Come, See, Overcome !—— O poor Cæfar !

M O D E L Y (humming a tune.)
You think I am difconcerted now ?

B E L M O U R

Why really I fhould think fomething of that
kind.

M O D E L Y.

You never were more miftaken in your life. ——
Egad 'tis a fpirited girl. She and Sir John Dorilant were certainly born for one another. I have a
good

good mind to take compaffion of them, and let
them come together. They muft and fhall be
man and wife, and I will e'en go back to Araminta.

BELMOUR.
Thou haft a moft aftonifhing affurance.

MODELY.
Hufh!——fhe is coming this way——get into
your hole again and be dumb.——Now you fhall
fee a fcene of triumph indeed.

BELMOUR.
Have a care, Cæfar, you have the Britons to
deal with.   [*Retires.*

Enter ARAMINTA.

ARAMINTA.
What, are they gone? and my wretch here by
himfelf?—O that I could diffemble a little!—I will,
if my heart burfts for it.——O, Mr. Modely,
I am half afhamed to fee you ;—but my brother
has figned thofe odious writings.

MODELY.
Then thus I feize my charmer.

ARAMINTA.
Agreeable rafcal!——Be quiet, can't you, you
think one fo forward now.

MODELY.
I cannot, will not be reftrained, when the dear
object of my wifhes meets me with kind compliance in her eyes and voice!—To-morrow!——
'Tis an age, why fhould we wait for that? To-
night, my angel, to-night may make us one; and
the fair profpect of our halcyon days even from
this hour begin.

ARA-

ARAMINTA.

Who would not think this fellow, with his blank verſe now, was in earneſt? But I know him tho-roughly:——Indeed Mr. Modely, you are too pref-fing, marriage is a ſerious thing. Beſides, you know, this idle buſtle betwixt my brother and Cælia, which you ſeem to think me ignorant of, and which you, in ſome meaſure, tho' undeſignedly I dare ſay, have occaſioned, may obſtruct us a little.

MODELY.

Not at all, my dear; an amuſement *en paſſant*; the meer raillery of gallantry on my ſide, to oblige her impertinent mother (who, you know, has a *penchant* for Sir John herſelf) was the whole in-ſignificant buſineſs. Perhaps, indeed, I was ſome-thing blameable in it.

ARAMINTA.

Why really I think ſo, in your ſituation. But are you ſure it went no farther? nothing elſe paſſed between you?

MODELY.

Nothing in nature.

ARAMINTA.

Dear me, how miſtaken people are. I cannot ſay that I believed it; but they told me, that you had actually propoſed to marry her, that the girl was near conſenting, and that the mother was your friend in the affair.

MODELY.

The mere malice, and invention of lady Bever-ley.

ARAMINTA.

And there is not a word of truth in it then?

MODELY.

Not a ſyllable——You know my ſoul is yours.

K
ARA-

ARAMINTA.

O thou villain!—I thought to have kept my temper, and to have treated you with the contempt you deferve; but this infolence is intolerable. Can you imagine that I am a ftranger to your proceedings? a deaf, blind ideot?—O I could tear this foolifh heart, which, cheated by its paffion, has encouraged fuch an infult.—How, how have I deferved this treatment?   [*Burfting into tears:*

MODELY (greatly alarmed.)

By holy faith!—by every power above! you, and you only are the paffion of my foul.—May every curfe ——

ARAMINTA.

Away, deceiver—thefe tears are the tears of refentment. My refolution melts not in my eyes. 'Tis fixed, unalterable! You might imagine from the gayety of my temper, that it had its levity too. But know, Sir, that a woman who has once been duped, defies all future machinations.

MODELY.

Hear me, madam——nay, you fhall hear me.——

ARAMINTA.

Shall!---infufferable infolence!--Go, Sir; for any thing which regards me, you are free as air, free as your licentious principles. Nor fhall a thought of what I once efteemed you, difturb my future quiet. There are men who think me not contemptible, and under whofe protection I may fhelter my difgrace.——Unhand me—this is the laft time I fhall probably ever fee you; and I may tell you in parting, that you have ufed me cruelly; and that Cælia knows you as perfectly as I do.

[*Exit Araminta.*

MODE-

MODELY (ſtands confounded.)

Enter BELMOUR.

BELMOUR.

Cæſar aſhamed!——and well he may i'faith.
Why, man, what is the matter with you? Quite
dumb? quite confounded? Did not I always tell
you that you loved her?

MODELY.

I feel it ſenſibly.

BELMOUR.

And I can tell you another ſecret.

MODELY.

What's that?

BELMOUR.

That ſhe loves you.

MODELY.

O that ſhe did!

BELMOUR.

Did!——Every word, every motion of paſſion
through her whole converſation betrayed it involuntarily. I wiſh it had been otherwiſe.

MODELY.

Why?

BELMOUR.

Becauſe I had ſome thoughts of circumventing
you. But I find it will be in vain. Therefore
purſue her properly, and ſhe is yours.

MODELY.

O never, Belmour, never.—I have ſinned beyond
a poſſibility of pardon. That ſhe did love me, I
have had a thouſand proofs, which like a brain-

less ideot I wantonly trifled with.   What a piti-
ful rascal have I made myself?.

BELMOUR.

Why in that I agree with you; but don't despair, man; you may still be happier than you deserve.

MODELY.

With what face can I approach her? Every cir-
cumstance of her former affection, now rises in
judgment against me.   O Belmour! she has
taught me to blush.

BELMOUR.

And I assure you it becomes you mightily.

MODELY.

Where can I apply?—How can I address her?
All that I can possibly do, will only look like a
mean artificial method, of patching up my other
disappointment.

BELMOUR.

More miracles still! She has not only taught
you to blush, but has absolutely made a man of
honour of you l

MODELY.

Raillery is out of season.

Enter a SERVANT.

SERVANT.

Mrs. Araminta, Sir, desires to speak with you.

MODELY (eagerly.)

With me?

SERVANT.

No, Sir, with Mr. Belmour.

BELMOUR.

With me?

SER-

SERVANT.

Yes, Sir.

BELMOUR.

Where is she?

SERVANT.

In the close walk by the house, Sir.

BELMOUR.

And alone?

SERVANT.

Entirely, Sir.

BELMOUR.

I wait upon her this instant. [*Exit Servant.*

MODELY.

Belmour, you shall not stir.

BELMOUR.

By my faith but I will, Sir.

MODELY.

She said there were men to whom she could fly for protection. By my soul she intends to propose herself to you.

BELMOUR,

And if she does, I shall certainly accept her offer.

MODELY.

I'll cut your throat if you do.

BELMOUR.

And do you think to fright me by that? I fancy I can cut throats as well as other people. Your servant. If I cannot succeed for myself, I'll speak a good word for you. [*Exit Belmour.*

MODELY.

What can this mean?——I am upon thorns till I know the event. I must watch them.——No, that is dishonest.——Dishonest! How virtuous does a real passion make one!——Heigh ho!

[*Walks about in disorder.*

He seems in great haste to go to her. He has turned

turned into the walk already.——That abominable old fashioned cradle work makes the hedges so thick, there is no seeing through them.——An open lawn has ten thousand times the beauty, and is kept at by less expence by half.——These cursed unnatural chairs are always in the way too.

[*Stumbling against one of the garden chairs.*

What a miserable dog am I?——I would give an arm to know what they are talking about.——We talk of female coquettes! By my soul we beat them at their own weapons!——Stay——one stratagem I may yet put in practice, and it is an honest one.——The thought was lucky.——I will about it instantly. Poor Modely!——How has thy vanity reduced thee?

END of the FOURTH ACT.

A C T V.

S C E N E *continues.*

A R A M I N T A *and* B E L M O U R.

A R A M I N T A.

YOU find, Mr. Belmour, that I have feen your partialities, and like a woman of honour I have confeſſed my own. ⸱ Your behaviour to your friend is generous beyond comparifon, and I could almoſt join in the little ſtratagem you propofe, merely to fee if he deferves it.

B E L M O U R.

Indeed, madam, you miſtake him utterly: Vanity is his ruling vice; an idle affectation of fuccefs among the ladies, which makes fools admire, and boys envÿ him, is the maſter paſſion of his giddy heart. The fevere checks he has met with to-day, have fufficiently opened his underſtanding ; and the real poſſeſſion of one valuable woman, whom he dreads to lofe, ⸱ will foon convince him how defpicable his folly has made him.

A R A M I N T A.

I am afraid, Mr. Belmour, a man who has half his life been purfuing bubbles, without perceiving their infignificance, will be eafily tempted to re-

fume

fume the chace. The poffeffion of one reality
will hardly convince him that the reft were fhadows.
And a woman muft be an ideot indeed, who thinks
of fixing a man to herfelf after marriage, whom
fhe could not fecure before it. To begin with in-
fenfibility, O fie, Mr. Modely.

BELMOUR.

You need not fear it, madam; his heart——

ARAMINTA.

Is as idle as our converfation on the fubject. I
beg your pardon for the comparifon; as I do, for
having fent for you in this manner. But I thought
it neceffary that both you and Mr. Modely fhould
know my real fentiments, undifguifed by paffion.

BELMOUR.

And may I hope you will concur in my propofal?

ARAMINTA.

I don't know what to fay to it, it is a piece of
mummery which I am ill fuited for at prefent. But
if an opportunity fhould offer, I muft confefs I
have enough of the woman in me, not to be infen-
fible to the charms of an innocent revenge.——But
this other intricate bufinefs, if you can affift me in
that, you will oblige me beyond meafure. There are
two hearts, Mr. Belmour, worthy to be united! Had
my brother a little lefs honour; and fhe a little lefs
fenfibility—— But I know not what to think of it.

BELMOUR.

In that, madam, I can certainly affift you.

ARAMINTA.

How, dear Mr. Belmour?

BELMOUR.

I have been a witnefs, unknown to Cælia, to
fuch a converfation, as will clear up every doubt
Sir John can poffibly have entertained.

ARA-

ARAMINTA.

You charm me when you fay fo.——As I live, here comes my brother. ——— S$_{t}$a$_{y}$; is not that wretch Modely with him ? He is actually. What can his affurance be plotting now ?—Come this way, Mr. Belmour ; we will watch them at a diftance, that no harm may happen between them, and talk to the girl firft ! The monfter !—— *Exeunt.*

Enter SIR JOHN DORILANT *and* MODELY.

MODELY. (Entering and looking after Araminta and Belmour.)

They are together ftill !———
But let me refume my nobler felf.

SIR JOHN.

Why will you follow me, Mr. Modely ? I have purpofely avoided you.——My heart fwells with indignation.———I know not what may be the confequence.

MODELY.

Upon my honour, Sir John———

SIR JOHN.

Honour, Mr. Modely ! 'tis a facred word. You ought to fhudder when you pronounce it. Honour has no exiftence but in the breaft of truth. 'Tis the harmonious refult of every virtue combined.— You have fenfe, you have knowledge; but I can affure you, Mr. Modely, tho' parts and knowledge, without the dictates of juftice, or the feelings of humanity, may make a bold and mifchievous member of fociety even courted by the world, they only, in my eye, make him more contemptible.

MODELY.

This I can bear, Sir John, —— becaufe I have deferved it.

SIR JOHN.

You may think, perhaps, it is only an idle affair with a lady, what half mankind are guilty of, and what the conceited wits of your acquaintance will treat with raillery. Faith with a woman! ridiculous! — But let me tell you, Mr. Modely, the man who even slightly deceives a believing and a trusting woman, can never be a man of honour.

MODELY.

I own the truth of your assertions. I feel the aweful superiority of your real virtue. Nor should any thing have dragged me into your presence, so much I dreaded it, but the sincerest hope of making you happy.

SIR JOHN.

Making me happy, Mr. Modely! —— You have put it out of your own power.———[*Walks from him, then turns to him again.*] —— You mean, I suppose, by a resignation of Cælia to me.

MODELY.

Not of Cælia only, but her affections.

SIR JOHN.

Vain, and impotent proposal!

MODELY.

Sir John, 'tis not a time for altercation.———
By all my hopes of bliss here and hereafter, you are the real passion of her soul.———Look not so unbelieving: by heaven 'tis true; and nothing but an artful insinuation of your never intending to marry her, and even concurring in our affair, could ever have made her listen one moment to me.

SIR JOHN.

Why do I hear you? —— O Mr. Modely, you touch my weakest part.

MODE.

MODELY.

Cherish the tender feelings, and be happy.

SIR JOHN.

Is it possible that amiable creature can think and talk tenderly of me? I know her generosity; but generosity is not the point.

MODELY.

Believe me, Sir, 'tis more; 'tis real unaffected passion. Her innocent soul speaks through her eyes the honest dictates of her heart. In our last conference, notwithstanding her mother's commands; notwithstanding, what I blush to own, my utmost ardent solicitations to the contrary, she persisted in her integrity, tore the papers which left her choice free, and treated us with an indignation which added charms to virtue.

SIR JOHN.

O these flattering sounds!———Would I could believe them!

MODELY.

Belmour, as well as myself, and lady Beverley, was a witness of the truth of them. I thought it my duty to inform you, as I know your delicacy with regard to her. And indeed I would in some measure endeavour to repair the injuries I have offered to your family, before I leave it for ever.———O Sir John, let not an ill-judged nicety debar you from a happiness, which stands with open arms to receive you. Think what my folly has lost in Araminta; and, when your indignation at the affront is a little respited, be blest yourself; and pity me. —— [*As he goes out, he still looks after Araminta and Belmour.*]——— They are together still; but I will go round that way to the house.

Exit Modely.

SIR

SIR JOHN.

What can this mean? —— He cannot intend
to deceive me ; he feems too fincerely affected. —
I muft, I will believe him. The mind which fufpects injuftice, is half guilty of it itfelf.——Talks
tenderly of me? Tore the parpers? Treated them
with indignation? Heavens! what a flow of tender joy comes over me! —— Shall Cælia then be
mine? How my heart dances! O! I could be
wondrous foolifh!—Well, Jonathan.

Enter STEWARD.

STEWARD.

The gentleman, Sir ——

SIR JOHN.

What of the gentleman? I am ready for any
thing.

STEWARD.

Will wait upon your honour to-morrow, as you
are not at leifure.

SIR JOHN.

With all my heart. Now or then, whenever he
pleafes.

STEWARD.

I am glad to fee your honour in fpirits.

SIR JOHN.

Spirits! Jonathan! I am light as air.—Make a
thoufand excufes to him; —— but let it be to-
morrow, however, for I fee lady Beverley coming
this way.

STEWARD.

Heaven blefs his good foul! I love to fee him
merry. [*Exit*,

Enter

Enter LADY BEVERLEY.

LADY.

If I don't interrupt you, Sir John ——

SIR JOHN.

Interrupt me, madam? 'tis impoſſible.

LADY.

For I would not be guilty of an indecorum, even to you.

SIR JOHN.

Come, come, lady Beverley, theſe little bickerings muſt be laid aſide. Give me your hand, lady. Now we are friends [*Kiſſing it.*] —— How does your lovely daughter?

LADY.

You are in mighty good humour, Sir John; perhaps every body may not be ſo.

SIR JOHN.

Every body muſt be ſo, madam, where I come; I am joy itſelf.

"The jolly god that leads the jocund hours!"

LADY.

What is come to the man? —— Whatever it is, I ſhall damp it preſently. —— [*Aſide.*] ——
Do you chuſe to hear what I have to ſay, Sir John?

SIR JOHN.

You can ſay nothing, madam, but that you conſent, and Cælia is my own. —— Yes, you yourſelf have been a witneſs to her integrity. Come, indulge me, lady Beverley. Declare it all, and let me liſten to my happineſs.

LADY.

I ſhall declare nothing, Sir John, on that ſubject: what I have to ſay is of a very different import. —— In ſhort, without circumlocution, or

4

any

any unneceſſary embarraſſment to entangle the affair, I and my daughter are of an opinion, that
it is by no means proper for us to continue any
longer in your family.

S I R - J O H N.

Madam !

L A D Y.

This is what I had to declare, Sir John.

S I R J O H N.

Does Cælia, madam, deſire to leave me ?

L A D Y.

It was a propoſal of her own.

S I R J O H N.

Confuſion !

L A D Y.

And a very ſenſible one too, in my opinion. For
when people are not ſo eaſy together, as might be
expected, I know no better remedy than parting.

S I R J O H N. (Aſide.)

Sure, this is no trick of Modely's, to get her
away from me ?—He talked too himſelf, of leaving my family immediately.—I ſhall relapſe again.

L A D Y.

I find, Sir John, you are ſomewhat diſconcert-
ed : but, for my part ——

S I R J O H N.

O torture !

L A D Y.

I ſay, for my part, Sir John, it might have
been altogether as well, perhaps, if we had never
met.

S I R J O H N.

I am ſorry, madam, my behaviour has offended
you, but ————.

Enter

Enter ARAMINTA, CÆLIA, *and*
BELMOUR.

ARAMINTA. (*to Cælia as she enters.*)
Leave the house indeed! Come, come, you shall
speak to him.——— What is all this disorder for?
Pray, brother, has any thing new happened?———
That wretch has been before-hand with us—(*Aside
to Belmour.*)

LADY.

Nothing at all, Mrs. Araminta; I have only
made a very reasonable proposal to him, which he
is pleased to treat with his and your usual in-
civility.

SIR JOHN.

You wrong us, madam, with the imputation.
——— (*After a pause, and some irresolution, he goes up
to Cælia.*)——— I thought, Miss Beverley, I had already given up my authority, and that you were
perfectly at liberty to follow your own inclinations.
I could have wished, indeed, to have still assisted
you with my advice; and I flattered myself that
my presence would have been no restraint upon
your conduct. But I find it is otherwise. My
very roof is grown irksome to you, and the innocent pleasure I received in observing your growing
virtues, is no longer to be indulged to me.

CÆLIA.

O Sir, put not so hard a construction upon what
I thought a blameless proceeding. Can it be won-
dered at, that I should fly from him, who has
twice rejected me with disdain?

SIR JOHN.

With disdain, Cælia?

CÆLIA.

CÆLIA.

Who has withdrawn from me even his parental tendernefs, and driven me to the hard neceffity of avoiding him, left I fhould offend him farther.

I know how much my inexperience wants a faithful guide ; I know what cruel cenfures a malicious world will pafs upon my conduct ; but I muft bear them all. For he who might protect me from myfelf, protect me from the infults of licentious tongues, abandons me to fortune.

SIR JOHN.

O Cælia !——have I, have I abandoned thee ? ———Heaven knows my inmoft foul how it did rejoice but a few moments ago, when Modely told me that your heart was mine !

ARAMINTA.

Modely !——Did Modely tell you fo ?—— Do you hear that, Mr. Belmour ?

SIR JOHN.

He did, my fifter, with every circumftance which could increafe his own guilt, and her integrity.

ARAMINTA.

That was honeft, however.

SIR JOHN.

I thought it fo, and refpected him accordingly. O he breathed comfort to a defpairing wretch ! but now a thoufand thoufand doubts crowd in upon me. He leaves my houfe this inftant ; nay, may be gone already. Cælia too is flying from me,—— perhaps to join him, and with her happier lover, fmile at my undoing !——(*Leans on Araminta.*)

CÆLIA.

I burft with indignation !——Can I be fufpected
of

of fuch treachery? Can you, Sir, who know my every thought, harbour fuch a fufpicion?—O madam, this contempt have you brought upon me. A want of deceit was all the little negative praife I had to boaft of, and that is now denied me.

[Leans on Lady Beverley.

LADY.

Come away, child.

CÆLIA.

No, madam. I have a harder tafk ftill to perform. *[Comes up to Sir John* To offer you my hand again under thefe circumftances, thus defpicable as you have made me, may feem an infult. But I mean it not as fuch.—O Sir, if you ever loved my father, in pity to my orphan ftate, let me not leave you. Shield me from the world, fhield me from the worft of misfortunes, your own unkind fufpicions.

ARAMINTA.

What fooling is here? Help me, Mr. Belmour. ——There, take her hand. — And now let it go if you can.

SIR JOHN (grafping her hand.)

O Cælia! may I believe Modely? Is your heart mine?

CÆLIA.

It is, and ever fhall be.

SIR JOHN.

Tranfporting extacy!—— *[Turning to Cælia.*

LADY.

I fhould, think Sir John, a mother's confent —— tho' Mrs. Araminta, I fee, has been fo very good to take that office upon herfelf.

M   SIR

SIR JOHN.

I beg your pardon, madam; my thoughts were too much engaged. —— But may I hope for your concurrence?

LADY.

I don't know what to say to you; I think you have bewitch'd the girl amongst you.

ARAMINTA.

Indeed, lady Beverley, this is quite preposterous. ——Ha!—— He here again!——Protect me, Mr. Belmour.

Enter MODELY.

MODELY.

Madam, you need fly no where for protection: you have no insolence to fear from me. I am humbled sufficiently, and the post-chaise is now at the door to banish me for ever.— My sole business here is, to unite that virtuous man with the most worthy of her sex.

ARAMINTA (half aside.)

Thank you for the compliment——Now, Mr. Belmour.

LADY.

You may spare yourself that trouble, cousin Modely; the girl is irrecoverably gone already.

MODELY.

May all the happiness they deserve attend them!

[*Going, then looks back at Araminta.*
I cannot leave her.

SIR JOHN.

Mr. Modely, is there nobody here besides, whom you ought to take leave of?

MODE-

M O D E L Y.

I own my parting from that lady *(to Araminta)* fhould not be in filence ; but a conviction of my guilt ftops my tongue from utterance.

A R A M I N T A.

I cannot fay I quite believe that ; but as our affair may make fome noife in the world, for the fake of my own character, I muft beg of you to declare before this company, whether any part of my conduct has given even a fhadow of excufe for the infult I have received. If it has, be honeft, and proclaim it.

M O D E L Y.

None by heaven ; the crime was all my own, and I fuffer for it juftly and feverely——with fhame I fpeak it, notwithftanding the appearances to the contrary, my heart was ever yours, and ever will be.

A R A M I N T A.

I am fatisfied ; and will honeftly confefs, the fole reafon of my prefent appeal was this, that where I had deftined my hand, my conduct might appear unblemifhed.   [*Gives her hand to Belmour.*

M O D E L Y.

Confufion!——then my fufpicions were juft.

S I R J O H N.

Sifter !

C Æ L I A.

Araminta!

A R A M I N T A.

What do ye mean? What are ye furprized at ? ——The infinuating Mr. Modely can never want miftreffes any where. Can he, Mr. Belmour ? You know him perfectly.

MODE-

M O D E L Y.

Diftraction!——Knows me? Yes, he does know me. The villain! though he triumphs in my fufferings, knows what I feel!——You, madam, are juft in your feverity, from you I have deferved every thing; the anguifh, the defpair which muft attend my future life comes from you like heaven's avenging minifter!——But for him——

[*Sir John interpofes.*

O for a fword!————But I fhall find a time, and a fevere one.——Let me go, Sir John————

A R A M I N T A.

I'll carry on the farce no longer.——Rafh inconfiderate madman! The fword which pierces Mr. Belmour's breaft, would rob you of the beft of friends.——This pretended marriage, for it is no more, was merely contrived by him, to convince me of your fincerity.——Embrace him as your guardian angel, and learn from him to be virtuous.

B E L M O U R.

O madam, let me ftill plead for him. Surely when a vain man feels himfelf in the wrong, you cannot defire him to fuffer a greater punifhment.

A R A M I N T A.

I have done with fooling.—— You told me to-day, lady Beverley, that he would never return to me.

L A D Y.

And I told you at the fame time, madam, that if he did—you would take him.

A R A M I N T A.

In both you were miftaken.——Mr. Modely, your laft behaviour to Cælia and my brother, fhews a generofity of temper I did not think you capable

of

of, and for that I thank you. But to be serious on our own affair, whatever appearance your present change may carry with it, your transactions of to-day have been such, that I can never hereafter have that respect for you, which a wife ought to have for her husband.

SIR JOHN

I am sorry to say it, Mr. Modely, her determination is, I fear, too just. Trust to time however, at least let us part friends, and not abruptly. We should conceal the failings of each other, and if it must come to that, endeavour to find out specious reasons for breaking off the match, without injuring either party.

ARAMINTA.

To shew how willing I am to conceal every thing, now I have had my little female revenge, as my brother has promised us the fiddles this evening, Mr. Modely, as usual, shall be my partner in the dance.

MODELY.

I have deserved this ridicule, madam, and am humbled to what you please.

ARAMINTA.

Why then, brother, as we all seem in a strange dilemma, why may'nt we have one dance in the garden? it will put us in good humour.

SIR JOHN.

As you please, madam.—Call the fiddles hither. —Don't despair Mr. Modely. [*Half aside to him.*

LADY.

I will not dance, positively.

BELMOUR.

Indeed but you shall, madam; do you think I will be the only disconsolate swain who wants a partner? Besides, you see there are a few of us,

that

that we muſt call in the butler and the ladies maids even to help out the figure.

SIR JOHN.

Come, lady Beverley, you muſt lay aſide all animoſities. If I have behaved improperly to you to-day, I moſt ſincerely aſk your pardon, and hope the anxieties I have been under will ſufficiently plead my excuſe ; my future conduct ſhall be irreproachable.   [Turning to Cælia.

Here have I placed my happineſs, and here expect it. O Cælia, if the ſerioufneſs of my behaviour ſhould hereafter offend you, impute it to my infirmity ; it can never proceed from want of affection.

A heart like mine its *own* diſtreſs contrives,
And feels *moſt* ſenſibly the pain it gives ;
Then even its frailties candidly approve,
For, if it errs, it errs from too much love.

A   D A N C E.

E P I-

EPILOGUE.

Spoken before the DANCE,

By Mrs. YATES and Mr. PALMER, in the
Characters of ARAMINTA and MODELY.

ARAMINTA.

WELL, ladies, am I right, or am I not ?
    Should not this foolish passion be forgot ;
This fluttering something, scarce to be exprest,
Which pleads for coxcombs in each female breast ?
How mortified he look'd ! — and looks so still.

                           [Turning to Modely.
He really may repent —— perhaps he will. ——

MODELY.

Will, Araminta ? ——Ladies, be so good,
Man's made of frail materials, flesh and blood.
We all offend at some unhappy crisis,
Have whims, caprices, vanities, — and vices.
Your happier sex by nature was design'd,
Her last best work, to perfect humankind.
No spot, no blemish the fair frame deforms,
No avarice taints, no naughty passion warms
Your firmer hearts. No love of change in you
E'er taught desire to stray. ——

ARAMINTA.

                All this is true.

EPILOG

Yet stay; the men, perchance, will call it ſneer,
And ſome few ladies think you not ſincere.
For your petition, whether wrong or right,
Whate'er it be, withdraw it for to-night.
Another time, if I ſhould want a ſpouſe,
I may myſelf report it to the houſe:
At preſent, let us ſtrive to mend the age;
Let juſtice reign, at leaſt upon the ſtage.
Where the fair dames, who like to live by rule,
May learn two leſſons from the LOVER'S SCHOOL,
While Cælia's choice inſtructs them how to chuſe,
And my refuſal warns them to refuſe.

THE END.

ERRATA.

Page 9. l. 20. *for* you and I, *read* you and me
10. l. 4. *for* you and I, *read* you and me
15. l. 9. *for* a fellow, *read* fellow
l. the laſt but two, *for* ſhould you think, *read* you
    ſhould think
31. l. 19. *for* marry come up! *read* very fine truly!
40. l. 2. *for* you fight me, *read* you will fight me.
41. l. 15. *for* advice, *read* adviſe
l. 16. *for* lady's, *read* ladyſhip's
48. l. 4. *for* perſuad, *read* perſuade
61. l. 14. *for* you make, *read* you may make
75. l. laſt but one, *for* they are together ſtil, *read* I don't
    ſee them now
76. l. 5. *for* parpers, *read* papers
80. l. 11. *for* it did, *read* did it

CPSIA information can be obtained
at www.ICGtesting.com
Printed in the USA
BVHW04*1045170918
527708BV00015B/1867/P